SEQUENCING STORIES

# Making a Valentine

MEG GAERTNER

**The Child's World®**
childsworld.com

Published by The Child's World®
1980 Lookout Drive • Mankato, MN 56003-1705
800-599-READ • www.childsworld.com

Photographs ©: Light Field Studios/Shutterstock
Images, cover (left), cover (middle left),
cover (middle right), cover (right), 3 (left), 3
(right), 5, 6, 9, 10, 13, 14, 17, 18, 21

ISBN 9781503835139
LCCN 2018963103

Printed in the United States of America
PA02425

## About the Author

Meg Gaertner is a children's
book author and editor who
lives in Minnesota. When not
writing, she enjoys dancing and
spending time outdoors.

# CONTENTS

# It Is Valentine's Day!

Valentine's Day is today! Mia wants to make a card for her mom. She wants to tell her mom that she loves her.

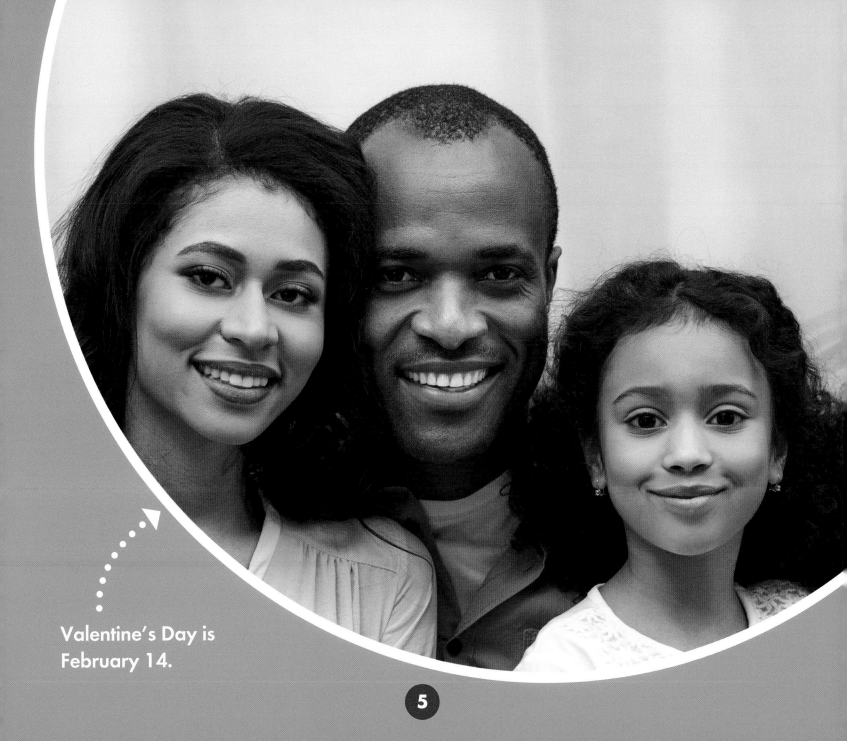

Valentine's Day is
February 14.

People also use lace, ribbons, and glitter to make cards.

Yesterday, Mia and her dad bought supplies. They got lots of colored paper. They also got markers, scissors, and a glue stick. Now they are ready to create their Valentine's Day cards.

**Fun Fact**

Valentine's Day is named after Saint Valentine. He helped people marry in secret.

First, Mia cuts a white sheet of paper in half. This makes the paper the right size for her Valentine's Day card.

Use scissors carefully when you cut paper.

9

Folding the paper in half helps make the heart an even shape.

Then, Mia takes another sheet of paper. She folds it in half. This will make it easier to cut out paper hearts.

Next, Mia draws one half of a heart along the **crease**. She takes her scissors and cuts along the line. When she unfolds the **cutout**, she has a whole heart!

Many Valentine's Day cards have hearts on them.

13

Have you ever made
someone a card?

Mia immediately shows her dad the paper heart. He is happy for her! While she has been working, her dad has been making his own card.

Mia and her dad share the glue stick. They borrow it from each other from time to time. Mia glues the paper heart inside the card. She does not have much time left. Her mom will be coming home soon!

You can also use tape or regular glue to make a card.

What else could Mia
add to her card?

18

To finish her card, Mia writes her Valentine's Day message. She draws a picture on the front of the card. Just then, Mia's mom arrives home!

Mia finished her card just in time!
Mia gives her mom the Valentine's
Day card. It says, "I love you, Mom!"
Her mom gives her a big hug. It is a
very happy Valentine's Day!

How do you show people you care about them?

21

# Glossary

**crease** (KREESS) A crease is the ridge made in a piece of paper when it has been folded. Mia drew one half of a heart along the crease in the paper.

**cutout** (KUT-owt) A cutout is a shape that has been cut from paper. Mia made the cutout of a heart.

**marry** (MA-ree) To marry someone is to go through a ceremony in which you promise to spend your life with that person. Saint Valentine helped other people marry each other.

# To Learn More

## BOOKS

Lettice, Jenna. *The 12 Days of Valentine's*.
New York, NY: Random House, 2017.

Mathiowetz, Claire. *Valentine's Day Crafts*.
Mankato, MN: The Child's World, 2017.

Trueit, Trudi Strain. *Valentine's Day*.
New York, NY: Children's Press, 2014.

## WEBSITES

Visit our website for links about making a Valentine:
**childsworld.com/links**

*Note to Parents, Teachers, and Librarians: We routinely verify our Web links to make sure they are safe and active sites. So encourage your readers to check them out!*

# Index